THE TRUTH ABOUT
DOLPHINS

THE TRUTH ABOUT DOLPHINS

Maxwell Eaton III

A NEAL PORTER BOOK
ROARING BROOK PRESS
NEW YORK

ISBN: 978-1-62672-668-0
Library of Congress Control Number:2017957306

Our books may be purchased in bulk for promotional, educational, or business use. Please
contact your local bookseller or the Macmillan Corporate and Premium Sales Department at
(800) 221-7945 ext. 5442 or by e-mail at MacmillanSpecialMarkets@macmillan.com.

First edition, 2018
Book design by Jennifer Browne

Printed in China by Shaoguan Fortune Creative Industries Co. Ltd.,
Shaoguan, Guangdong Province

1 3 5 7 9 10 8 6 4 2

This is a dolphin.

Dolphins look like fish. But they aren't!

Dolphins are actually mammals,
like humans, bears, and cats.

They breathe air.

They're warm-blooded.
(That means they have about the same body temperature no matter how cold or warm their surroundings are.)

And they give birth to live young (not eggs).

When a baby dolphin is born, it usually comes out of its mother tail-first.

Then its mother nudges it to the surface
for its first breath of air.

Finally, like all mammals, the young
dolphin drinks milk from its mother.

Dolphins come in all different shapes, sizes, and colors.

And they can be found in every ocean and sea in the world. From warm tropical waters . . .

SPINNER DOLPHINS ARE NAMED FOR THEIR ABILITY TO SPIN AS THEY LEAP THROUGH THE AIR.

They hunt in groups, called pods, by using their eyes, ears, and one very special ability . . .

The amount of time it takes for the clicks to bounce back tells the dolphin the size, shape, and position of the object.

Ack! Faster!

This seems like a safe spot.

3. THE SOUNDS THEN BOUNCE OFF AN OBJECT AND RETURN AS ECHOES.

4. THE ECHOES TRAVEL THROUGH CAVITIES IN THE DOLPHIN'S LOWER JAW AND TO ITS EARS.

Doing this hundreds of times per second allows them to paint a picture of their surroundings. Even in the dark!

Dolphins are excellent communicators.

Each dolphin has a unique whistle that only it makes.

The whistle is like the dolphin's personal song or name. It helps dolphins recognize their friends.

Dolphins love to play!

All of this play and communication
helps dolphins work together
when hunting . . .

and watching out for sharks.

Dolphins do need to watch out for sharks, but their biggest threats are humans . . .

The problems are large, but you can help by learning about dolphins and then teaching others.

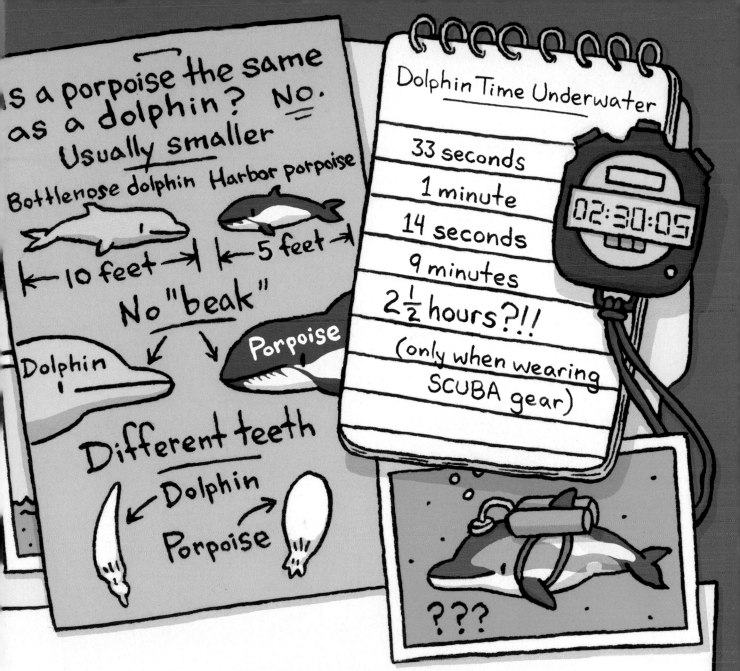

Is a porpoise the same as a dolphin? No. Usually smaller

Bottlenose dolphin   Harbor porpoise

10 feet   5 feet

No "beak"

Dolphin   Porpoise

Different teeth

Dolphin
Porpoise

Dolphin Time Underwater

33 seconds
1 minute
14 seconds
9 minutes
2½ hours?!!
(only when wearing SCUBA gear)

02:30:05

???

Further Research

TUCUXI-SIZED BOOKS

Is a Dolphin a Fish? Questions and Answers About Dolphins, Gilda Berger and Melvin Berger, illustrated by Karen Carr, Scholastic, 2001.

Dolphin Baby!, Nicola Davies, illustrated by Brita Granström, Candlewick Press, 2012.

ORCA-SIZED BOOKS

Whales, Dolphins, and Porpoises, Mark Carwardine, illustrated by Martin Camm, DK, 2002.

Whales and Dolphins in Question: The Smithsonian Answer Book, James G. Mead and Joy P. Gold, Smithsonian Institution Press, 2002.